# ELECTION

INSHAMAMULHAQ

**ISBN:** 9781312067318

# DEDICATION

I am dedicate to my family members for their unconditional support .

# ACKNOWLEDGMENT

I acknowledge to god for showing grace on me to educate.

I also acknowledge each and every person who give support and motivated me for book publishing.

# CONTENTS

# PRINCIPLE

An electrol voting expresses the principle of equal rights to each and every citizen of country to representing in voting. It's nature of democracy and political equality, helps them to decide their proportional representation.

Every Democratic and Republic country has It's own electrol system and reforms . Elections make a fundamental contribution to democratic governance.

Elections enable voters to select leaders and to hold them accountable for their performance in office. Accountability can be undermined.

The Basic Principles of Democracy are Citizen Participation, Equality, Political Tolerance, Accountability, and Transparency. People around the world have defined the core values through elections required for a democratic government. Elections also reinforce the stability and help legitimacy in the country

Elections take place regularly in any democracy. There are more than 100 countries in the world in which elections take place to choose people's representatives.

The mechanism by which people can choose their representatives at regular intervals and change them whenever they want to is called an election.

# SYSTEM OF ELECTION

The electoral system is one of the main sources of institutional diversity among democratic countries

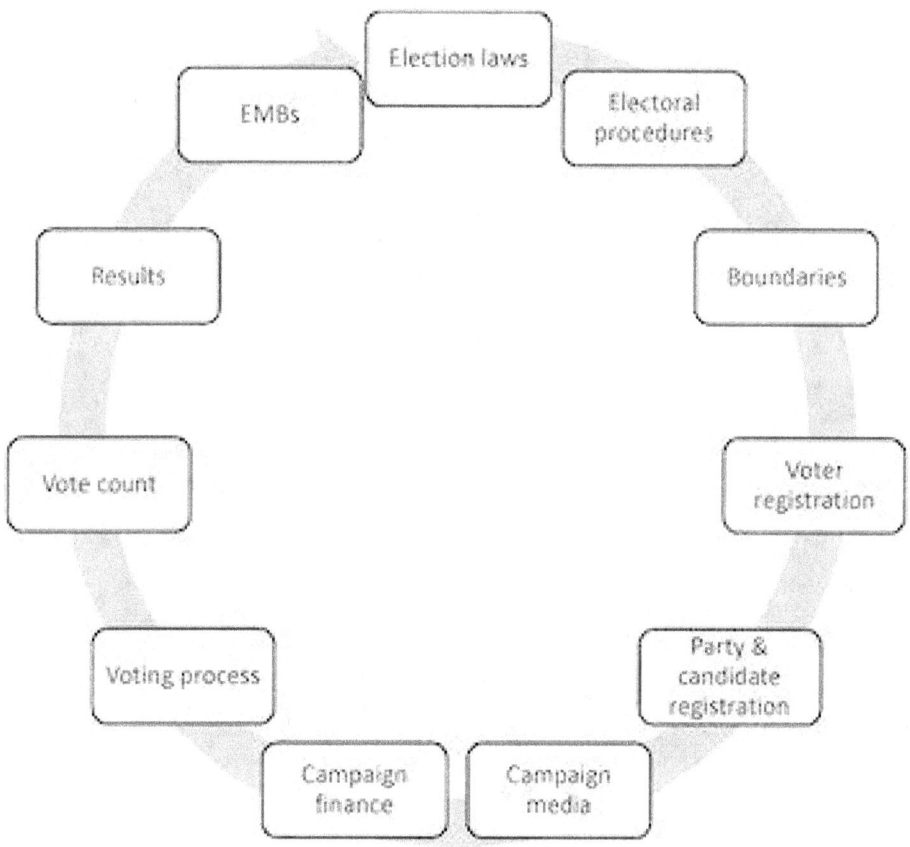

An electrol  SYSTEM which varies from  one country  to  another  country . There are also separate criteria that can be used to evaluate each system as a whole. Each criterion is best understood as a spectrum The country is split up into separate geographical areas/known as constituencies, and the electors can cast one vote each for a candidate, Electoral systems are divided into three broad families: plurality/majority systems, proportional systems (PR), and mixed systems. However, some electoral systems do not fit into any particular family

Party-list proportional representation is the single most common electoral system and is used by 80 countries, and involves voters voting for a list of candidates proposed by a party. Public perceptions may be misleading, however, especially where governments muzzle criticism or where arcane technical processes like gerrymandering determine the outcome.

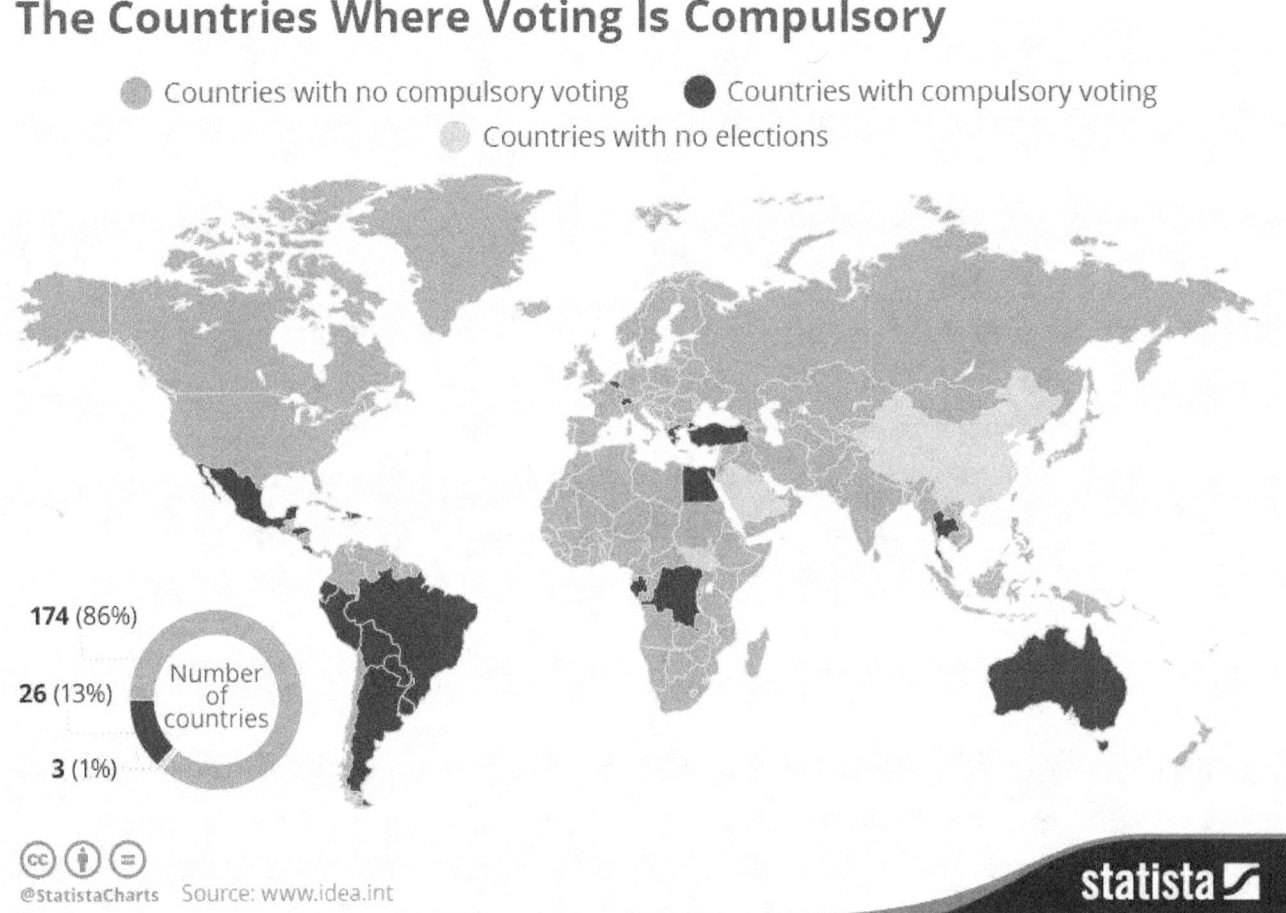

## The Countries Where Voting Is Compulsory

● Countries with no compulsory voting    ● Countries with compulsory voting
● Countries with no elections

174 (86%)

26 (13%)    Number of countries

3 (1%)

@StatistaCharts    Source: www.idea.int

statista ◢

Courtesy ; statista

# TYPES OF ELECTROL SYSTEM

We've tried to show how democratic different systems are. We have not included every country and we've not compared the UK to dictatorships or to nations with very weak democracies. The Democracy Map is also supplemented with some key electoral facts to illuminate how democratic such nations are.

It is also important to remember that states often have multiple democratic system and different systems can be used at different levels. For example, although the UK Parliament uses FPTP, the Scottish Assembly is elected using the Additional Member System (AMS).

For the purposes of this analysis we have simplified matters by focusing on the dominant legislature. This is obviously not perfect; for in some countries (e.g. France, USA and Russia) elected presidents have significant power that is distinct from and in addition to the main legislative chamber.

There are also many different alternatives to FPTP and the umbrella term Proportional Representation (PR) does not exhaust all our options. We have ranked electoral systems into 7 different groups, starting with the most democratic options:

**PROPORTIONAL REPRESENTATION** : Each party composes a list of potential candidates for each multi-member districts and the number of those elected from each list is representative of the vote. There are many different forms of PR including the STV (Single Transferable Vote) system. Within our definition of Proportional Representation we've grouped together the different forms that PR can take.

**Alternative Vote (AV)** - Voters rank candidates in order of their preference. If a candidate wins over 50% they automatically win the seat. If there is no victory by majority, the candidate with the fewest 1st preference votes is knocked out and their 2nd preferences are distributed to the other candidates. This process is continued until one candidate has the support of over 50% of the votes.

**Mixed System** - Mixed System is also known as an Additional Members System (AMS) and is a system that combines both PR and FPTP. There are two ballot papers. One is to vote for a local representative. The other is a list of major Vote

**Two-Round System (2RS)** - Voters mark their preferred candidate. If they win over 50%, then they win the election. If not, a second vote is conducted between the two candidates who came first. The candidate who wins the second ballot is then elected.

**Parallel System (PS)** - This is a hybrid of systems which, on our analysis is a hybrid of FPTP and PR. Unlike mixed systems like AMS the PR component of a parallel system does not compensate for any disproportionality within the FPTP system.

**First Past the Post (FPTP)** - Voters pick a local representative (who usually belongs to a party). The candidate with the most votes will then go into government to form a state legislature.

**Party Block Voting (PBV)** - Voters have 1 vote where they vote for a block list of candidates. The party with the most votes wins the entire list of candidates.

Our criteria for ranking these systems were these four factors:

Representative - The balance of the vote is genuinely translated into the balance of seats in the legislative chamber.

Multi-party system - The voting system encourage a genuine choice between varied candidates.

Few wasted votes - The system provides as much value as possible to all votes.

In the text below we provide more background information about these systems, their impact and examples of places where the system is used.

# 1. PROPORTIONAL REPRESENTATION

Proportional representation system is most commonly used around the world

Each party composes a list of potential candidates for each multi-member district and the number of those elected from each list is representative of the vote. There are many different forms of PR including the Single Transferable Vote (STV) system.

On our analysis of PR is the most representative electoral system. This is because the purpose of PR is to try and reflect how the population has voted as accurately as possible. This means that PR ranks well against all our criteria, particularly regarding representation, multi-party system and few wasted votes. This is because smaller parties can gain representation.

This consequently means that there are few wasted votes. Representation of smaller parties is crucial for democracy in order to provide scrutiny to the ruling parties. However, the challenge may be choosing which format to take as there are various forms in which PR is utilised.

PR encourages the development for a multi-party system. Fringe parties can rise to prominence based on the public agenda. Austria for example in its most recent legislative election, had 5 parties receive between 71 seats and 15 seats. The Green party who had previously managed 0 seats in the prior election, increased their total to 26. This highlights how PR can respond to public opinion. On the other hand, the Green Party struggle to gain representation in the UK because of the FPTP electoral system.

They consistently in the past few elections only managed to get 1 seat. This has amounted to around 0.2% of seats but they have received a greater percentage of the vote. Whilst it was just at 3.2% in the last election, if voters had faith in a system whereby their vote wouldn't be wasted, then they would have more faith and vote for fringe parties.

PR allows this to happen. Whilst the electorate are aware that they may not win, they can be confident that voting for them means that they can at least gain some form of parliamentary representation. Latvia is an example of a new democracy that has gone down the PR route. It has proven to produce a multi-party system. In the most recent parliamentary election, 7 parties gained seats ranging from 23 to 8 seats. This highlights the equal split and level of multi-representation.

BY our criteria PR only relative weakness is that it weakens the constituency link by relying on larger constituencies. However, what PR does mirror how the  constituency has actually voted. This means that there is a greater possibility that the voter helps elect a candidate who they have voted for.

A supposed attraction of FPTP is that it does provide a strong constituency link. However this is something of an illusion. As documentaries like 'Tory boy' highlight people's apathy towards their local MP. But, this is largely because of neglect from their MP. A system like PR would mean that MPs would have to fight for their seat and not take the constituents for granted. This is because they are more susceptible to change given that there are a greater number of seats per constituency.

One  could argue that there are in fact wasted votes in a PR system. Mark Rutte's VVD party has led the government since 2010 despite never receiving

26% of the vote. However, there is a far greater equal split in terms of representation in the Dutch legislature.

The 2021 election showed 17 parties gaining representation in the House of Representatives. Even parties with who received around 1% of the vote gained a seat in the House. This shows that your vote under PR has more meaning and even if your preferred party doesn't win, they can still form some sort of representation in the legislature. This is vital in a proper functioning democracy in order to achieve proper scrutiny of ruling parties.

Various forms of proportional representation exist, including the following:

In a party-list system, the elector votes for a party's list of candidates instead of a single candidate. Each party then receives a share of the seats proportional to the share of votes it received.

In a single transferable vote (STV) system, voters rank their choice of candidates on the ballot instead of voting for just one candidate. In an additional-member system, each elector casts two votes instead of one. On a double ballot, the elector chooses a candidate

| PARTY | Percentage of the vote | Initial seats (% vote x 200) | Remaining seats (% vote x (200-184) | Total seats | Percentage of seats |
|-------|-----------------------|------------------------------|--------------------------------------|-------------|---------------------|
| A | 42 | 84 | 7 | 91 | 46.5 |
| B | 30 | 60 | 5 | 65 | 32.5 |

| PARTY | Percentage of the vote | Initial seats (% vote x 200) | Remaining seats (% vote x (200-184) | Total seats | Percentage of seats |
|-------|------------------------|------------------------------|-------------------------------------|-------------|---------------------|
| C | 20 | 40 | 4 | 44 | 22 |
| D | 4 | – | – | – | – |
| E | 4 | – | – | – | – |
| Total | 100 | 184 | 16 | 200 | 100 |

**Examples**: Czech Republic, Serbia, Sweden, Colombia

## ALTERNATIVE VOTE (AV)

ALTERNATIVE VOTING (AV), also called ranked-choice voting or instant runoff, and also known as the alternative vote, transferable vote, ranked-choice voting (RCV), single-seat ranked-choice voting, or preferential voting. Voters rank candidates in order of their preference. If a candidate wins over 50% they automatically win the seat. If there is no victory by majority, the candidate with the fewest 1st preference votes is knocked out and you then look towards the 2nd preferences and so on.

A core advantage of AV is that it permits a multi-party system. Voters have to take interest in various parties to assess where their preferential votes are going. There are also few wasted votes as if an MP does not receive a majority then the second round of voting comes into play.

This also means that smaller parties have a higher chance of gaining some form of representation. However, if a party were to win 51% of the vote, then the remaining votes would be wasted in that constituency.

This can lead to many wasted votes. Indeed, the multi-party system can be jeopardised too given that larger parties attempt to strike up deals with smaller parties.

This gives too much leverage to larger parties meaning that they can manipulate smaller parties. Whilst voters may take greater notice of smaller parties when they are choosing their different preferences, they may base these opinions on how they have coalesced with larger parties.

An advantage of AV is that an MP has to win a majority. This means you are less likely to get MPs who don't care for their constituents and live for a large quantity of their time abroad (as can happen in the UK) for they need to ensure they are getting the majority of support from constituents.

In this aspect, constituents are electing candidates for whom they actually vote. It is also an effective way to ensure that a majority is reached. Indeed, there won't always be a majority winner in any system but, this attempts to ensure that if voters' first preference votes aren't chosen then at least their alternative preferences may be given support.

There are two types of AV systems:

1. Alternative Vote

2. Alternative Vote (Plus)

The AV Plus system differs from the traditional type of Alternative Vote System in that it includes a party-list component. Similar to the AV system, with AV Plus, voters are asked to rank individual candidates in order of preference. They must also select a party from the party-list column. The party-list votes are then distributed to represent each party's share of the votes proportionally.

The AV Plus system is not currently being used anywhere in the world. For that reason, we will focus on the more widely used type, Alternative Vote system,

AV is a less democratic system than PR given that it ultimately not representative as PR

There takes all approach means that ultimately there isn't as great representation as there is under PR. Indeed, an MP can be elected without winning a majority on the first round. This ultimately means that an MP doesn't necessarily represent the interests of their constituents.

In Australia smaller parties have helped to form the centre-right alliance of the Liberal-National Coalition'. Australia has in effect become a two-party system with the Liberal-National Coalition competing against Labour. In principle, AV should encourage voters to take greater interest in their alternative preferences. But, in practice this is not proving the case. In the last 3 elections in Australia, apart from the two largest parties, no other party has won more than 1 seat in parliament

Example of an alternative voting system is its use in Australia. First introduced in 1918 to replace the FPTP system and address the problem of vote-splitting, Australia has been using the AV system ever since. It is the only major democracy to use the system.

Currently, Australia uses various preferential voting systems in nearly all of its elections, from the upper and lower houses to municipal, state, and federal legislatures.

# Voting flowchart

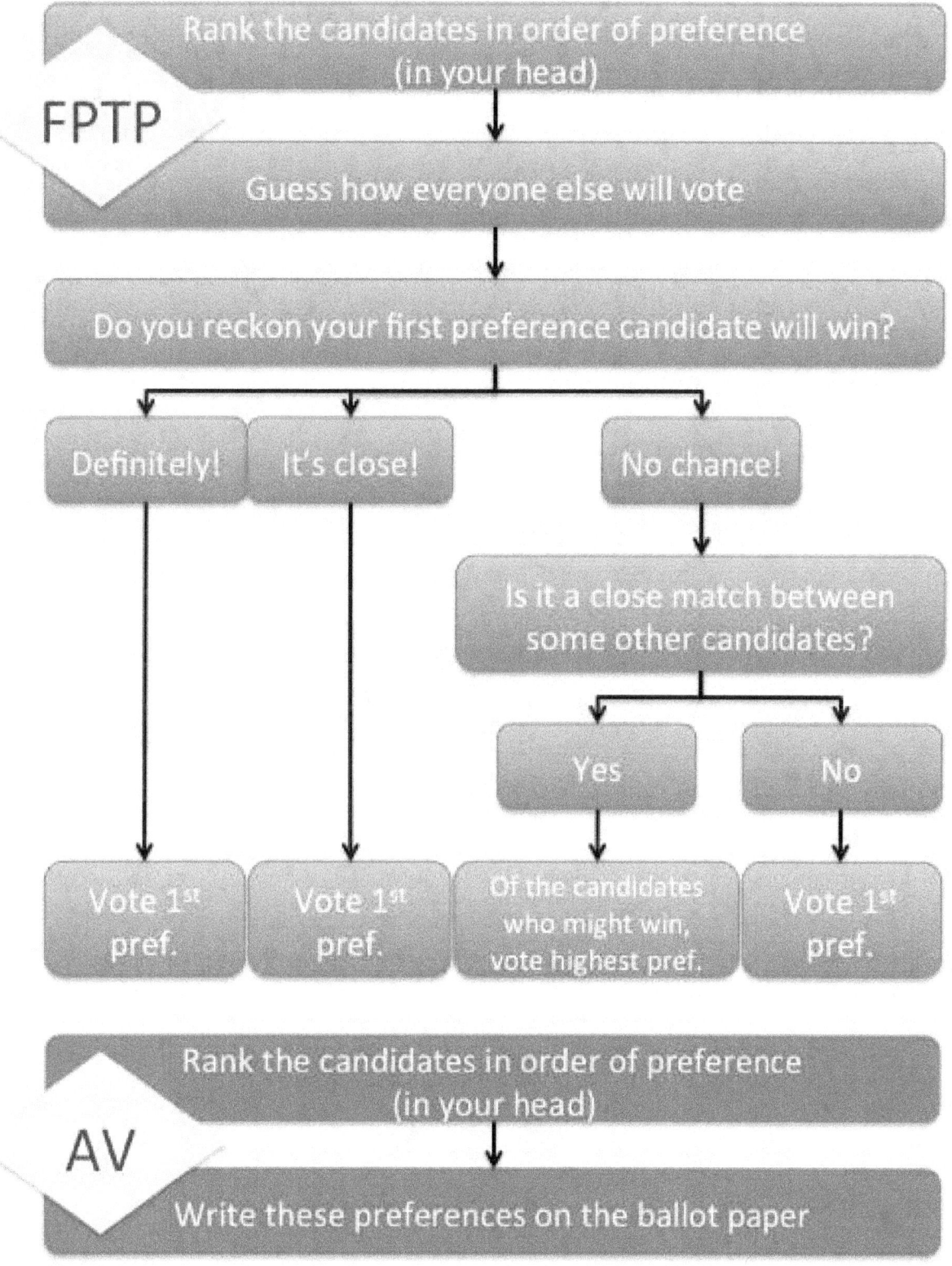

**FPTP**

Rank the candidates in order of preference (in your head)

Guess how everyone else will vote

Do you reckon your first preference candidate will win?

Definitely! | It's close! | No chance!

Is it a close match between some other candidates?

Yes | No

Vote 1st pref. | Vote 1st pref. | Of the candidates who might win, vote highest pref. | Vote 1st pref.

**AV**

Rank the candidates in order of preference (in your head)

Write these preferences on the ballot paper

The use of the AV system in Australia slightly varies depending on which state is holding the election. Australia uses Full Preferential Voting (FPV), which means that voters must rank in order of preference for each candidate on the ballot. South Wales uses the Optional Preferential Voting (OPV), whereby voters rank at least one or as many as all candidates in order of preference.

As a result of Australia's decision to employ preferential voting, the two-party system is less prevalent. More noteworthy, minor parties have gained more influence in Australian politics.

Papua New Guinea also used the AV system from 1964 to 1975.

Example: Australia ,Papua New guinea

# 3.. MIXED SYSTEM

Mixed System like electoral systems are described as a mixture of two principles of electoral system the Additional Member System (AMS) is a combination of PR and FPTP.

There are two ballot papers. One is to vote for a local representative. The other is a list of candidates who represent a party. In the district seats, the list seats are used to balance out the disproportionate results.

AMS is an attempt to try and maintain representation and a strong constituency link. In principle, it is a democratic idea. It means that there can be strong levels of representation nationally whilst also having local representation. Baston states

The local representative however ultimately doesn't have a great deal of authority. Also, the use of FPTP to elect a local MP is not representative of the overall vote for the respective constituency. AMS also stimulates internal conflict.

It creates resentment from the constituency MPs towards the party list MPs. It encourages parties to draw up a list of MPs to sneak people 'through the back door'. It is also becomes difficult when party-list MPs try to get involved in local issues. It generates uncertainty amongst the MPs and can create a degree of a power imbalance between the two.

However a positive of AMS is that voters have more choice and there is a multi-party system with voters often exercising that right. Voters can choose who they would like to represent them locally and nationally. This creates a multi-party system. Greater choice means greater political engagement too.

An issue with systems like FPTP is that fringe parties struggle to gain representation. In the UK for example, it can predominantly be viewed as a 2 party-system. This means that parties like the Green party, despite gaining more of the popular vote and gaining more relevance in political discourse, struggle to gain any sort of authority in parliament. The 2021 Federal election in Germany highlights how AMS can respond and reflect popular opinion.

The Green party won 118 seats in parliament in 2021 - something that is almost unimaginable in the UK. Indeed, Germany is a strong example of a multi-party system. Although the SDP and CDU/CSU did win the majority of votes between them, there is still significant representation in the makeup of the Reichstag from parties such as the Greens, FDP, ADF and the Left Party.

Mixed-member systems also often combine local representation most often single-member constituencies with regional or national multi-member constituencies representation, having multiple tiers. This also means voters often elect different types of representatives who might have different types constituencies.

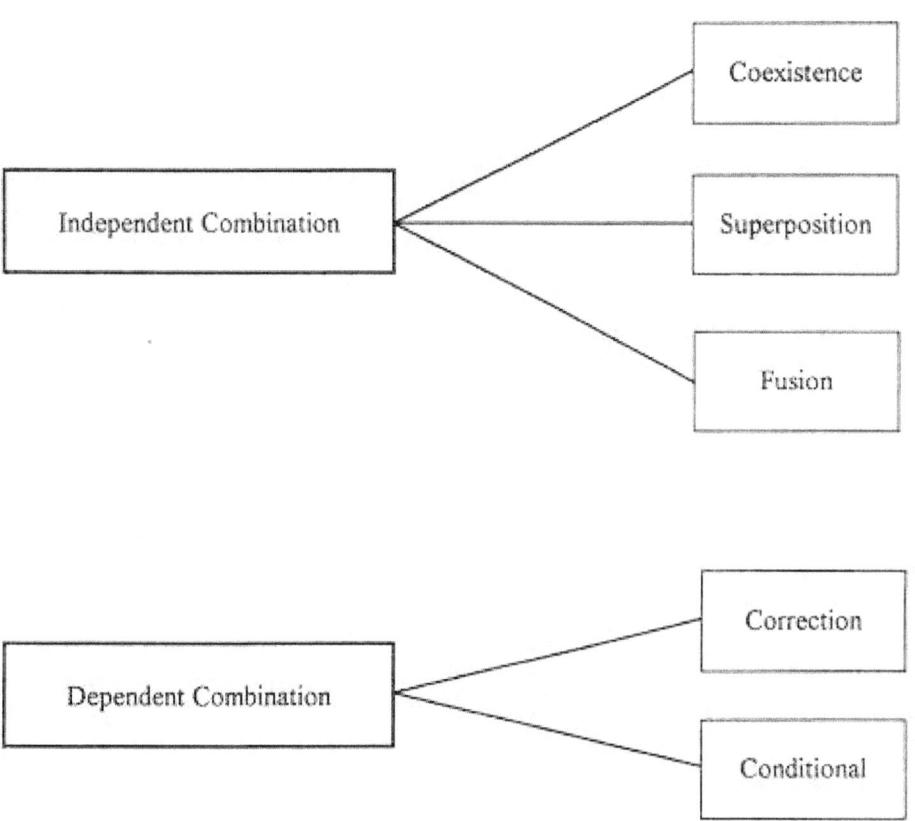

Some representatives may be elected by personal elections where voters vote
for candidates, and some by list elections where voter vote primarily
for electoral lists of parties more detailed classification  from the
compensatory/non-compensatory typology, a component systems relate to each

other, according to academic literature. Below is a table of different categories of mixed electoral systems based on the five main types identified by Massicotte & Blais.

According to their terminology, methods of compensation are referred to as compensation is referred to as correction, while another type of dependent combination exists, called the conditional relation between sub-systems.

Meanwhile, independent combinations mixed systems might have both local and national/regional tiers (called superposition), but some have only one at-large (national) tier, like the majority bonus system (fusion) or only a single tier for local/regional representation (called coexistence).

Examples: Germany, Scottish Parliament, Welsh Parliament

# 4. TWO-ROUND SYSTEM

The two-round system (TRS), also known as runoff voting, second ballot, or ballotage, is a voting method used to elect a single candidate, where voters cast a single vote for their preferred candidate

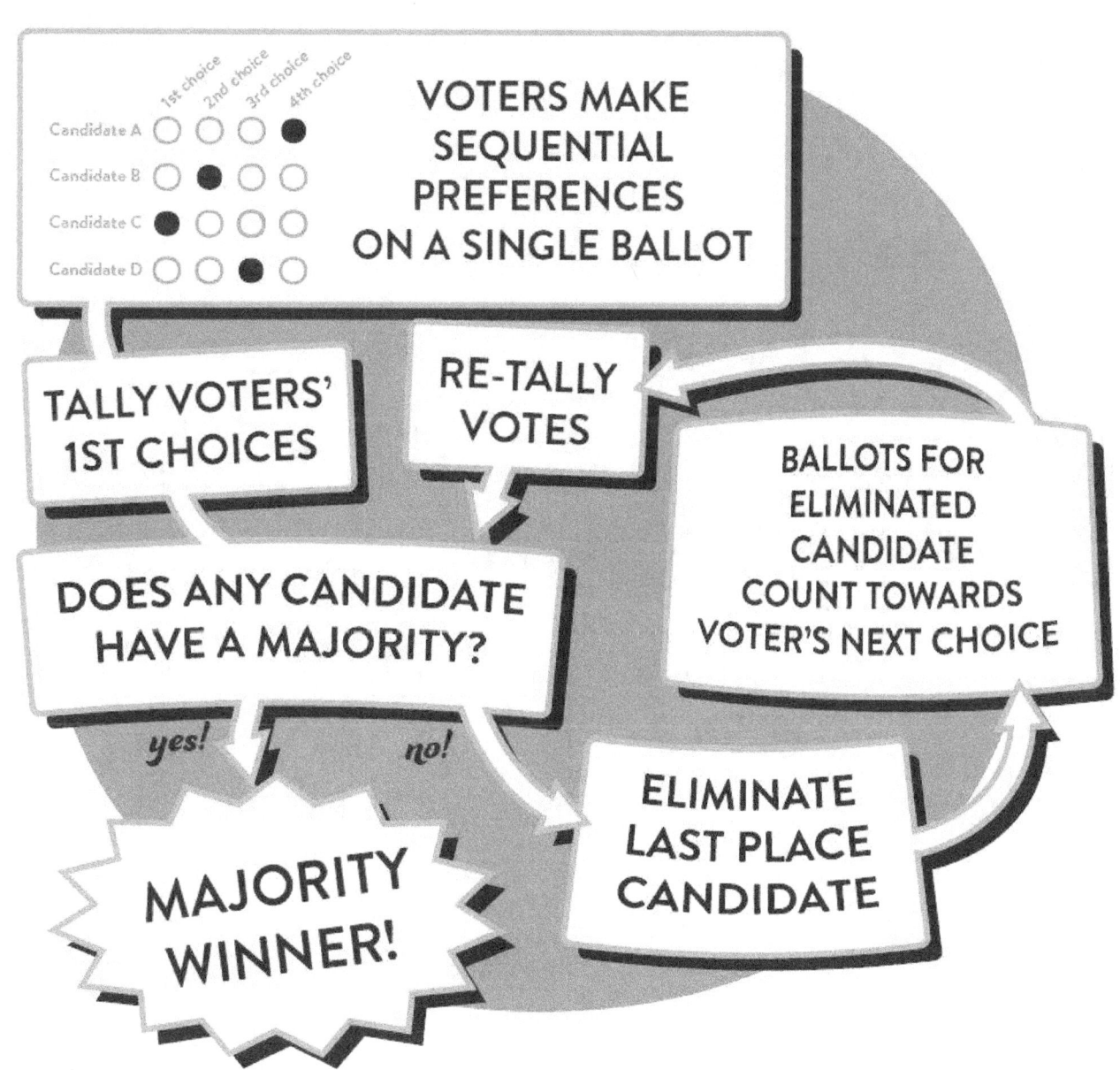

Two-Round voting system is rarely used in legislative chambers but is much more common as a system of electing a President. The core problem with Two-Round voting is that it is much harder for fringe parties to gain power.

France is a rarity in that it uses a Two-Round system for both its legislature and its presidential elections.

Despite receiving just 4% less of the vote than first place Macron in the first round of the voting in 2017, the Republican party because they were in third place wouldn't go to the second round. Indeed, this leads to a high amount of wasted votes of people who wanted to vote for the Republican party but in the Second Round had to settle for either voting for Macron or Le Pen. Similarly, La France Insoumise also received just 5% lower of the vote of Macron and didn't receive adequate representation.

In this 2017 election, En Marche! Topped the 1st round with 8.6million votes. They went to the next round with the 2nd place National Front. But The Republicans and La Republique En Marche received 7.2million votes and 7million votes respectively. This was evidently a very tight election that because of the system ended up between a choice between En Marche! And the National Front. This isn't a democratic choice given how the vote panned out in the first round of voting. One could argue however that a Two-Round system has allowed for parties like La Republique En Marche to enter the forefront of politics. Indeed, it is possible for fringe parties to gain relevancy.

However, in each election, there is still a question mark over how representative of the population as a whole. It may allow for fringe parties to rise but, representation may not be achieved for all of the relevant parties.

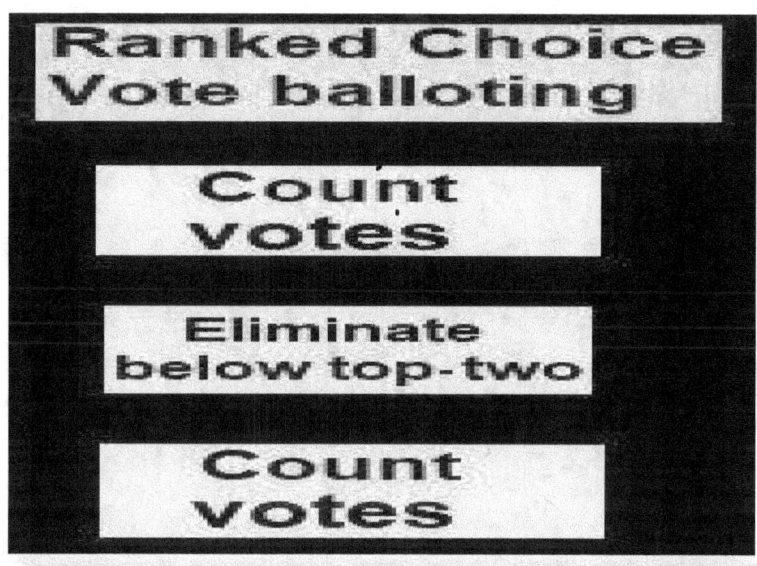

Moreover, whilst multi-party government may be possible, since the Second World War France has largely been dominated by two major parties. Although which parties these are has changed - and they are now far-right and centre parties. So effectively France still has a two-party system with other parties struggling to maintain relevancy. In 2017, Emmanuel Macron won just 24% of the vote in the first round. In an election with all the potential candidates present, for a party to win on just 24% of the vote is undoubtedly unrepresentative. He may have won 66% in the second round but fundamentally this highlights a further issue regarding a multi-party system. In the second round if the choice is only between two people that excludes smaller parties.

In the second round in 2017 in France, the choice was simply between Macron and the far-right candidates Le Pen. That means voters settle on one candidate often who they deem to be the least worst.

Moreover, France also produces disproportionate results. In 2017, the Presidential Majority coalition in the Second Round of voting received 49% of the vote but 60% of the seats. This is a similar representation as to how the voting occurs on a local level.

If a local representative doesn't receive a majority after the first round and goes to the second round, voters are therefore left with a choice of two parties they may have a lot of apathy towards. Indeed, they may still go out and vote but, a large number of the constituents will be disillusioned with their options. This is highlighted by how in the French legislative elections in 2017, 56% of the population abstained.

**Example:** France

## 5. Parallel Voting System

Parallel systems a form of mixed member majoritarian (semi-proportional) representation is used in the election of national parliaments can take multiple formats but the core principal is that it is 2 systems that elect 2 or more different chambers each. So, this may be a mix including proportional Representation, First Past the Post, Party block voting. Indeed , this is similar to AMS but the key difference is that with a Parallel Voting System there is no compensatory for disproportionality as a result of the district seat results. This means that proportionality of the vote is less likely and more likely to be distorted than under AMS.

Another disadvantage is that it creates a split between the two different sets of MPs. There is one group who are voted in by the electorate and are bound to their constituents. The other group, the election of party lists are accountable to their party leaders. This means that the elected officials are not wholly representative of the population, nor do they necessarily represent the desires of their party.

Parallel systems can certainly vary in terms of representation and some countries, and countries deviate in how many seats they assign for each system. Countries could assign 80% of the seats elected through PR and 20% through FPTP or vice versa. Votes can therefore be manipulated to suit a party's desires to their preferred electoral system. Andorra have a fair representation, as far as parallel systems, go with a 50/50 split.

A party that can gerrymander local districts can win more than its share of seats. So parallel systems need fair criteria to draw district boundaries.

Under Mixed member proportional representation a gerrymander can help a local candidate, but it cannot raise a major party's share of seats

Countries like Japan, Russia, and Thailand adopted a parallel system as a means by which incentives for greater party cohesiveness could be injected. The party is sure to elect the candidates at the top of its list, guaranteeing safe seats for the leadership. By contrast, under the MMP system a party that does well in the local seats will not need or receive any compensatory list seats, so the leadership has to run in the local seats

SM allows smaller parties that cannot win individual elections to secure some representation in the legislature; however, unlike in a proportional system they will have a substantially smaller delegation than their share of the total vote. It is also argued that SM does not lead to the degree of fragmentation found in party systems under pure forms of PR.

A criticism of proportional voting systems is that the largest parties need to rely on the support of smaller ones in order to form a government. However, smaller parties are still disadvantaged as the larger parties still predominate. In countries where there is one dominant party and a divided opposition, the proportional seats may be essential for allowing an effective opposition

Because the vote is split between constituencies and a list, there is a chance that two classes of representatives will emerge under a SM system: with one class beholden to their electorate seat, and the other concerned only with their party. The major critique of parallel systems is that they cannot guarantee overall proportionality, small parties may still be shut out of representation despite winning a substantial portion of the overall vote.

## Table 5. Countries Using Parallel Systems

| Country | No. of PR Seats | No. of Plurality/Majority (or other) Seats | Plurality/Majority (or other) System | Total No. of Seats |
|---|---|---|---|---|
| Andorra | 14 (50%) | 14 (50%) | PBV | 28 |
| Armenia | 90 (69%) | 41 (31%) | FPTP | 131 |
| Georgia | 77 (51%) | 73 (49%) | FPTP | 150 |
| Guinea | 76 (67%) | 38 (33%) | FPTP | 114 |
| Japan | 180 (38%) | 295 (62%) | FPTP | 475 |
| Korea, Republic of | 54 (18%) | 246 (82%) | FPTP | 300 |
| Lithuania | 70 (50%) | 71 (50%) | TRS | 141 |
| Monaco | 8 (33%) | 16 (67%) | BV | 24 |
| Pakistan | 70 (20%) | 272 (80%) | FPTP | 342 |
| Philippines | 58 (20%) | 233 (80%) | FPTP | 291 |
| Senegal | 60 (40%) | 90 (60%) | PBV | 150 |
| Seychelles | 9 (26%) | 25 (74%) | FPTP | 34 |
| Taiwan | 34 (30%) | 79 (70%) | FPTP | 107 |
| Tajikistan | 22 (35%) | 41 (65%) | TRS | 63 |
| Ukraine | 225 (50%) | 225 (50%) | FPTP | 450 |

**Examples**: Italy, Japan, Taiwan, Lithuania, Russia, and Argentina.

## 6. FIRST PAST THE POST (FPTP)

First Past the Post (FPTP) is the electoral system used in about a third of the world's countries. Voters pick a local representative (who usually belongs to a party). The candidate with the most votes will then go into government to form a state legislature.

An advantage of FPTP is that it can provide a strong constituency link. Steve Rotherham, an MP for Liverpool Walton, has campaigned for justice for the victims of the Hillsborough disaster. This highlights how an MP under FPTP can connect and represent local issues. A strong constituency link can be a beneficial factor of FPTP but it is far from a given.

The 2015 general election led to 331 MPs being elected without a majority of the vote. Under FPTP, many MPs are therefore elected without a majority of the vote - this means that it is not representative of the desires of the locals and leads to a lack of representation nationally too.

A 2015 Hansard survey found that 75% of people don't know who their local MP was. Indeed the recent issue of MPs having second jobs highlights how committed MPs are to their constituency. Geoffrey Cox has been spending time in the British Virgin Islands as part of his second job. This is hardly an exemplary example of FPTP showing a strong constituency link.

FPTP is therefore obviously not working in its supposed core positive which is to provide a strong constituency link if so many people have no evident connection to their MP. With a winner takes all approach to each constituency, this consequently leads to a significant number of wasted votes. In the 2019 general election, 14.5 million votes were cast to candidates who weren't elected. This accounted for 45% of the overall vote.

FPTP globally has just proven to be simply too unrepresentative. In 2014, the NDA Alliance in India won 62.5% of the seats on just 38.5% of the vote. Moreover, In 2016 Donald Trump received nearly 3 million fewer votes than Hilary Clinton yet, won more electoral college votes. This highlights the overwhelming influence of swing states such as the Rust Belt states in the U.S.

FPTP also means that there are huge number of wasted votes. In 2015, the Liberal Democrats won the seat of Southport on just 31% of the vote.

With a party having to gain the most votes in each constituency to win representation, it means that smaller parties need to ensure that they can get concentrated support in each constituency. In a system like PR, national support means that fringe parties can still gain representation. The need for concentrated support such as under FPTP means that fringe parties often don't garner support and those votes go wasted.

The winner takes-all-approach of FPTP means that fringe parties struggle to gain representation. Parties need high-levels of concentrated support which is why FPTP often generates two-party systems.

Fringe parties are consequently left behind. It also encourages gerrymandering. Gerrymandering is the redrawing of constituency or district lines. This is generally exploited by incumbent parties in order to increase their number of seats.

There are 2 key tactics when it comes to Gerrymandering. There is 'packing' which concentrates voters of the same party to reduce their influence in other more balanced and precarious districts.

There is also 'cracking' which involves spreading voters of a particular party out in order to reduce the concentration of support in a particular district.

The United States has had its districts drawn into abnormal lines in places such as Baltimore to manipulate an election to be swayed in a certain direction. As a consequence, this creates further misrepresentation of the vote.

**Example Riding:**
**Voters**

**Elected:**
**Blue MP**

**40%** blue voters
**30%** yellow voters
**20%** purple voters
**10%** salmon voters

This has become evident in the UK too. The Conservatives have recently proposed boundary changes which, off the basis of the vote on the 2019 election would increase their majority from 96 to 99. It may only be a slight increase but, it is an obvious manipulation of the vote to try and favour the ruling or incumbent party. It may only be a small step but, it is an example of how FPTP can encourage the subversion of democracy.

**Examples**: USA, UK, India.

# 7. PARTY BLOCK VOTE SYSTEM

Block voting or bloc voting refers to electoral systems in systems in which multiple candidates are elected at once and a group (voting bloc) of voters can force the system to elect only their preferred candidates.

Voters have 1 vote where they vote for a block list of candidates. The party with the most votes wins the entire list of candidates.

Party Block Voting's (PBV) core reason of being undemocratic is due to how unrepresentative of the vote. In the 1997 Djibouti general election, the RPP-FRUD party whilst it won a large majority of 78% of the vote, they won 100% of the seats. Party Block Voting involves the country being split into constituencies like under FPTP.

However, it differs in that you vote for a list of people but, it is still a winner takes all approach. Therefore, more candidates are elected to represent each constituency even if they don't represent the makeup of the electorate. In a sense, it is similar to PR in that a list of people are elected but, under PBV this list of people all represent the same party. A supposed benefit of PBV is that it enhances representation as it is supposed to encourage parties to draw up a list of candidates. This means that they can dictate the representational makeup of the list. However, in Mauritius for example this has proven not to be the case.

Just 11% of the current National Assembly are female for example. Opposition parties in Mauritius have proposed a change to the electoral system but as of yet have not had success. Opposition parties have proposed some sort of hybrid between PR and FPTP.

A core component of this movement is to try and increase the number of MPs to improve local representation in Mauritius. At the moment under a PBV system, the constituencies are too large meaning that the MPs aren't accountable to a local district. Therefore, a change to PBV has been proposed to try and improve local representation.

Under block voting, a slate of clones of the top-place candidate may win every available seat. A voter does have the option to vote for candidates of different political parties if they wish, but if the largest group of voters have strong party loyalty, there is nothing the other voters or parties can do to prevent a landslide.

While many criticize block voting's tendency to create landslide victories, some cite it as a strength. Since the winners of a block voting election generally represent the same slate or group of voters, there is greater agreement amongst those elected, potentially leading to a reduction in political gridlock

# MAJORITARIAN
## Party Block Vote

### Advantages

- Simple

- Encourages strong parties

- Can facilitate minority representation

### Criticisms

- Suffers from problems of FPTP, particularly disproportionality

**EXAMPLES** : Mauritius, Djibouti

# MODERN ELECTION STRATEGY

In the end of 20th century and beginning of 21st century elections are held through effective campaign and also with attractive manifesto and tactics. But nowadays elections are mainly depending upon private owned agencies around the globe.

The private agencies had played a major roles in modern elections. Some of the key features are

Building a campaign strategy

Identify goal and objectives

Policy analysis.

Identify your audience.

Identify your message.

Analyse your strengths and weaknesses.

Identify your tactics and activities.

Monitoring and evaluation.

## KEY ELECTION CAMPAIGN TACTICS

Having a firm grasp on the opposition is crucial to electoral success. Examine the advantages and disadvantages of your rivals as you study them. Check out what voters like about their campaigns. Are people of a certain age drawn to them, or are they acquiring supporters because of a specific action plan Take advantage of this knowledge to better target your campaign and win over more voters.

Create a report summarising the status of your rivals and the election scene as it stands now. You'll have a better idea of where you stand and how much work you need to put in to go ahead of the competition.

This method of political campaigning will illuminate your areas of strength and reveal the places where you can make the most progress When creating a financial plan for your upcoming political campaign, it's important to keep best political campaign strategies in mind.

We explain in detail how and when your campaign will spend its funds. Your campaign budget must be large enough to cover all the political campaign costs from launch to finish.

## GOALS AND OBJECTIVES

It is common for the members of a party to hold similar ideas about politics, and parties may promote specific ideological or policy goals. EACH AND EVERY PARTIES WHO FOUGHT IN THE ELECTION HAD THEIR GOAL TO TRIUMPH IN THE ELECTION through with their objectives it can be achieved only by hard work and also meet their requirements of people.

Tactics are the social action activities that you use to achieve your goals and objectives but the strategy is the sequencing of these in a logical and strategic way. List and detail the tactics required to achieve each campaign objective. Decide which tactics will deliver the greatest impact for the energy and resources you invest. Apply agreed tactics criteria to assess and justify tactics.

Political parties are essential institutions of democracy. By competing in elections parties offer citizens a choice in governance, and while in opposition they can hold governments accountable Before taking a political campaign to the voters, it is best to analysed the political landscape of your constituency. When u had a clear mission with long vision to achieve goals and their objectives.

## POLICY ANALYSIS

Policy analysis can be divided into two major fields: Analysis of existing policy, which is analytical and descriptive when attempts to explain policies and their development. Analysis for new policy, which is prescriptive it is involved with formulating policies and proposals .

They are many types of political policies which play a vital role in election

ORGANIZATIONAL POLICIES.

FUNCTIONAL POLICIES.

ORIGINATED POLICIES.

APPEALED POLICIES.

IMPOSED POLICIES.

GENERAL POLICIES.

SPECIFIC POLICIES and  IMPLIED POLICY.

People who care about important policy areas like the ones listed above should pay more attention to elections for state legislatures. Far less money is donated to and spent on elections for state legislatures, and many policy-motivated people focus almost exclusively on national elections.

Since state legislators feel pressure from their re-election, there is scope for influencing policy in state legislatures through traditional campaigning  not just voting, but donating to candidates and to groups that are active in the politics of state legislatures  changing the policy goals and preferences of state legislators, and decreasing the polarization of state legislatures, will likely require new people to run for state legislative office.

 Electoral pressures do not seem to change legislator platforms; the most logical explanation is that state legislators arrive in office with particular views, based on their own past experience and the groups from which they've received support. And they are unlikely to change these regardless of circumstances. Term limits have an important potential downside as a policy in state legislatures; they may lead legislators to shirk responsibilities when they cannot run for re-election.

There are many other arguments for and against term limits, so this evidence on its own is certainly not the final word on the policy, but it is an important thing to consider

# IDENTIFY VOTERS

Better funded campaigns are able to afford to poll the electorate to find potential supporters. Usually, a campaign starts with a "benchmark" poll at the beginning of the campaign. Large campaigns will even poll prior to that time in order to determine whether the candidate should run in the first place.

That's why some politicians form "exploratory committees." Once benchmark data has been obtained, a series of polls may be taken to track and adjust the campaign message and to chart momentum.

Polling also will give a candidate an idea which voters are persuadable and where they are located. Campaigns can spend a lot of money on polls and if a campaign can afford it, it is usually worth it.

Many ways to Identify voters

1. follow up for direct phone calls
2. Connect on their routine works
3. quick response to campaign developments

# STRENGTH AND WEAKNESS

Political parties have unified groups of people and helped them seek and achieve common goals. They have a tradition of participation in democratic government that is two centuries old.

Political parties have not, however, stemmed the decline in the number of people who vote. Many people view the primary elections as elimination contests that have little to do with political parties. TV ads and money from political action committees (PACs) seem to do more to persuade voters than the efforts of political parties.

Political parties today better reflect American society than they did a generation ago. Men and women from all ethnic and religious groups and from all walks of life participate in party caucuses and conventions. The primary system, whatever its defects, offers far more choices to voters than did the old party machines. This openness shows that political parties have had the strength and flexibility to adapt to changing times.

Main weaknesses of existing legal frameworks

Although a legal framework is necessary to regulate the influence of money in politics, it is not always sufficient. In many countries legal regimes governing campaign finance are riddled with loopholes and poorly enforced. It is difficult to enforce campaign finance regulation when laws are too complex, burdensome or vague to be implemented, or when oversight bodies are insufficiently resourced to carry out their duties.

## MONITORING AND EVALUATION

Monitoring and Evaluation (M&E) is a continuous management function to assess if progress is made in achieving expected results, to spot bottlenecks in implementation and to highlight whether there are any unintended effects from an campaigner project and its activities.

The processes of planning, monitoring and evaluation make up the Result-Based Management (RBM) approach, which is intended to aid decision-making towards explicit goals . Planning helps to focus on results that matter, while M&E facilitates learning from past successes and challenges and those encountered during implementation.

Elements of an M&E system which if developed together with all key stakeholders will encourage participation and increased ownership of a project/plan - Result Frameworks or logo frames ("RF"), which are tools to organize intended results, i.e. measurable development changes. RFs inform the development of the M&E plan and both must be consistent with each other the M&E plan, which contains a description of the functions required to gather the relevant data on the set indicators and the required methods and tools to do so.

The M&E plan is used to systematically organize the collection of specific data to be assessed, indicating roles and responsibilities of project/plan stakeholders. It ensures that relevant progress and performance information is collected processed and analyzed on a regular basis to allow for real-time, evidence-based decision-making;

The various processes and methods for monitoring (such as regular input and output data gathering and review, participatory monitoring, process monitoring) and for evaluation (including impact evaluation and thematic, surveys, economic analysis of efficiency and the Management Information System, which is an organized repository of data  to assist managing key numeric information related to the project/plan and the analysis

The numerical  system  has more assistance  in this  monitoring  process

.

Bottom line

   Now , modern days   political  parties  are mainly  depend  upon  private agencies  for elections. Each  and every   political party conducting  survey and also know  pulse of people.

This kind of election  campaign  and  working  are worsening  strength  of democracy